Notes on 'Brilliant Border Collies' colouring book:

There are 45 pages of unique artwork based on original, hand-drawn Susan Alison Border Collie designs.

The paper in this book is 60lb in weight ie crayons and pencils are your best bet for fab results. It's always a good idea to use a safety sheet underneath each page, whatever you're using.

Pictures are only printed on one side of the paper so that you can remove a page and display or frame it without losing the picture on the other side.

I have cropped and enlarged some of the designs to make different pictures and for those who prefer less intricate designs. They also allow experimentation with different colouring schemes. Some I've made into 6"x4" pictures – this is a nice size for framing, or for cutting out and sticking to the front of a greeting card blank. There are also some sheets of notepaper for that special person, and a page of bookmarks that can be coloured and laminated.

At the back of this book are a couple of pages for trying out your colours.

Most importantly – have fun!

To receive advance notice of new books you can subscribe
to my newsletter on any page of my website at:
www.SusanAlison.com

Or just email me at Susan@SusanAlison.com
It's always fab to hear from you!

SUSAN ALISON

BRILLIANT BORDER COLLIES

COLOURING BOOK

ISBN-13: 978-1537505572
ISBN-10: 1537505572

website and newsletter sign-up form: www.SusanAlison.com

CONTENTS

Only even numbers appear so that there is no number on the actual picture page. The title of the picture shows opposite the relevant design.

With thanks to the
Border Collie Trust GB

for all they do
for the dogs.

He was born to teach

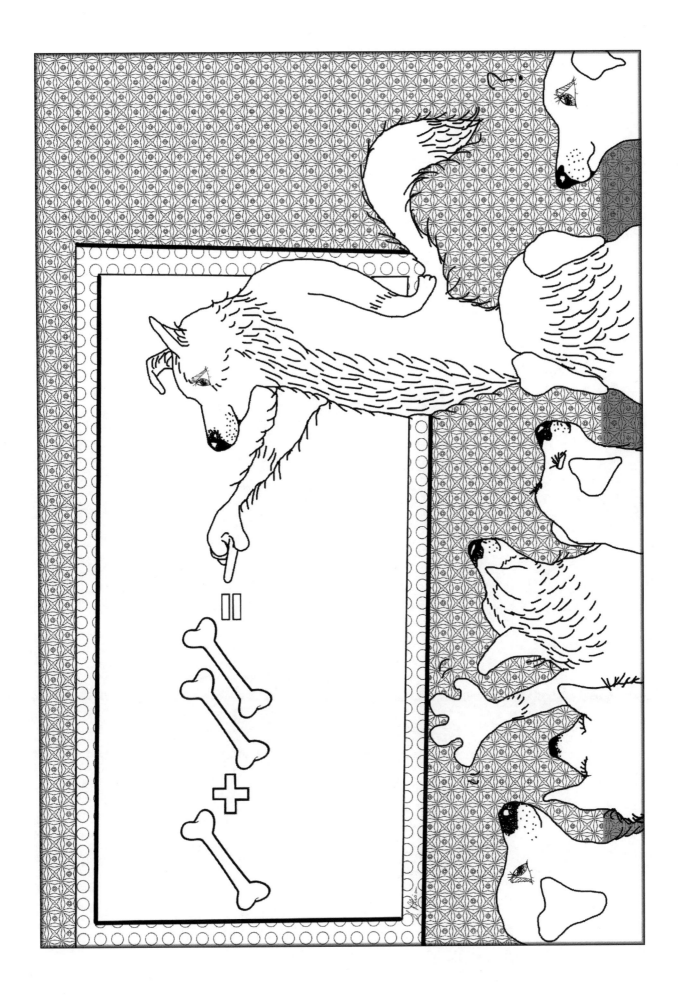

Science was his passion

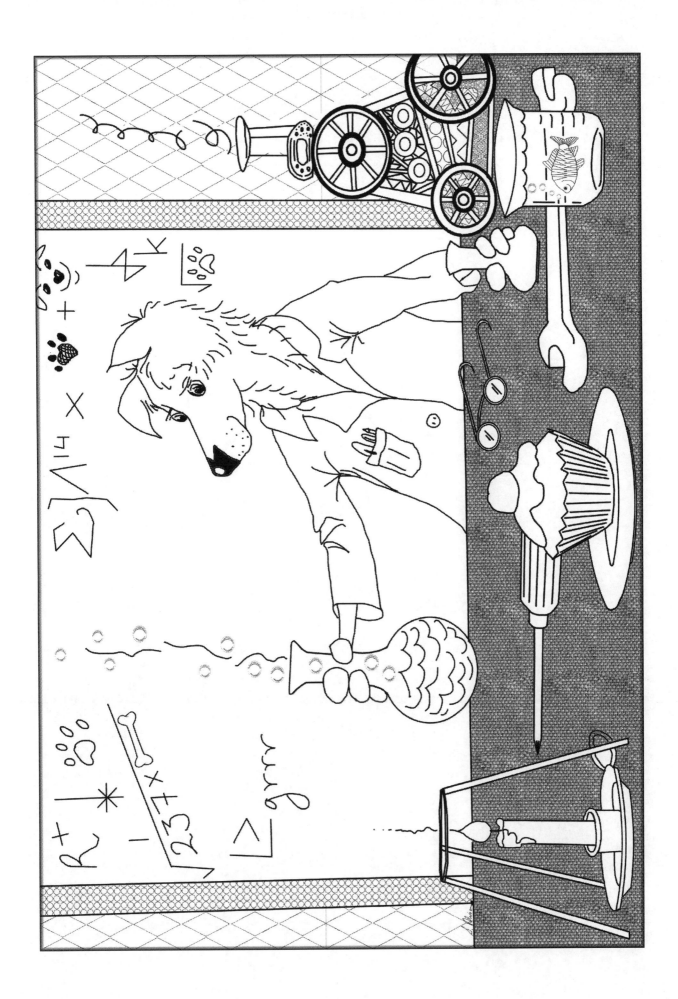

Butterflies galore

Butterflies galore

6"x4" – for framing or for a greeting card front

Or just for colouring!

Butterflies galore

(cropped and enlarged)

Stained glass – 'Eek! The sheep are out!'

Stained glass – 'Eek! The sheep are out!'

6"x4" – for framing or for a greeting card front

Or just for colouring!

Forget me not

Forget me not

6"x4" – for framing or for a greeting card front

Or just for colouring!

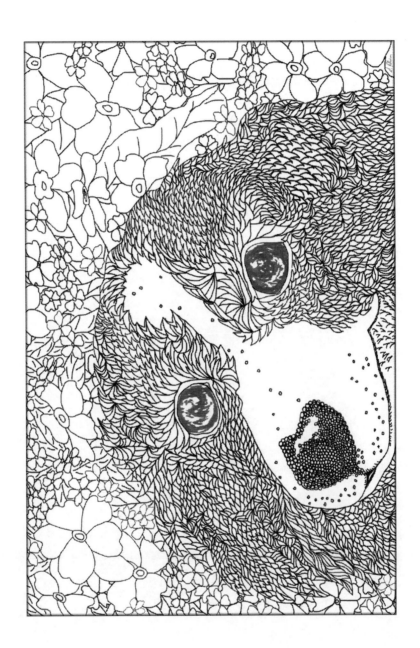

Deep sea dawg

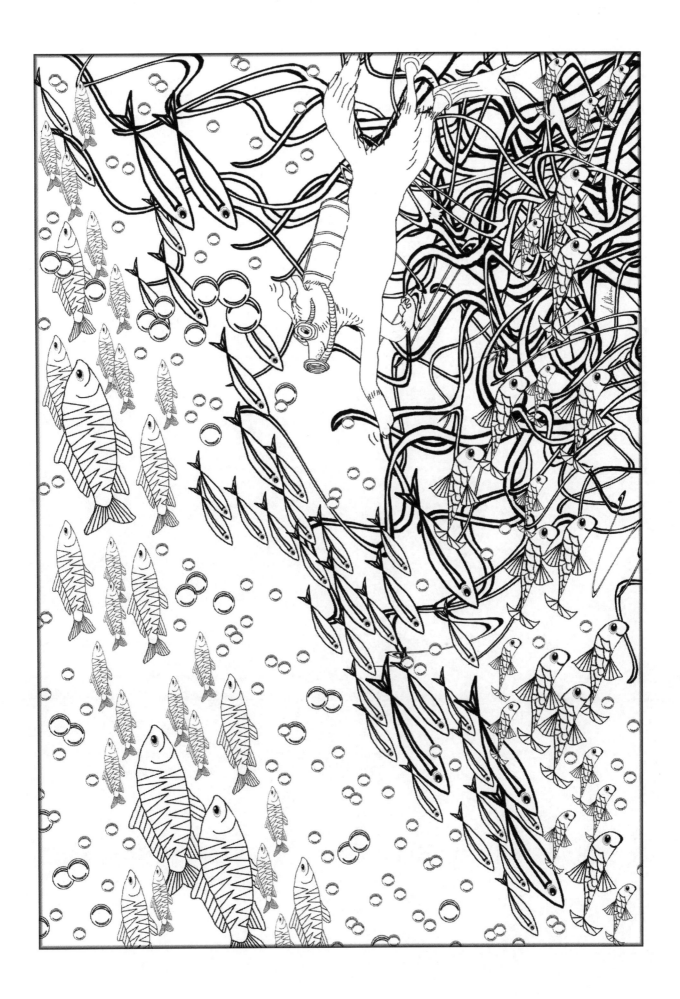

Deep sea dawg

(cropped and enlarged)

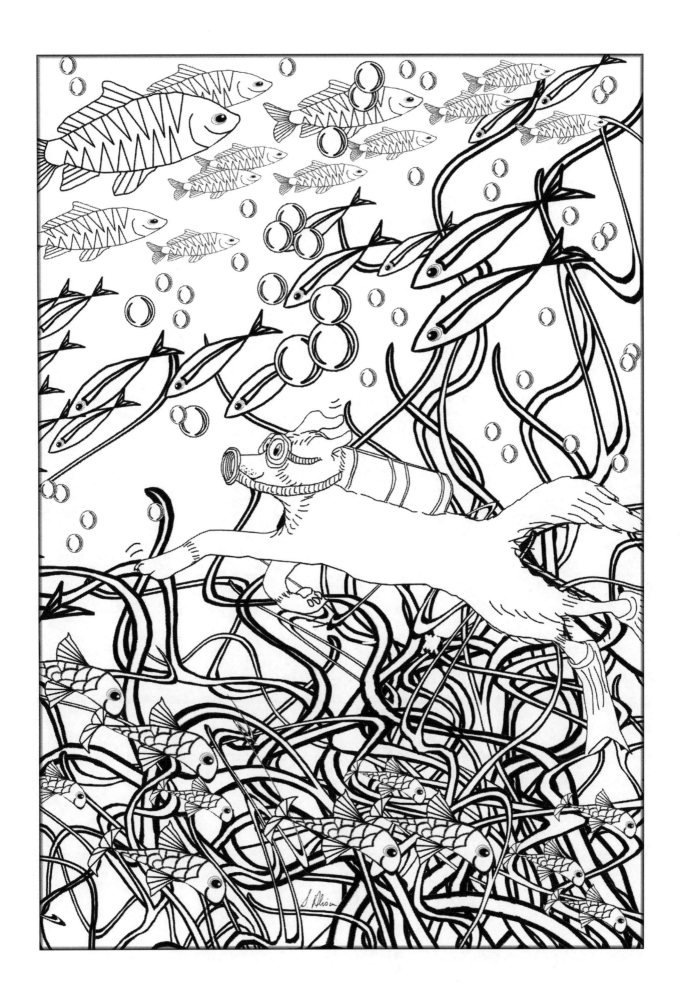

Deep sea dawg

6"x4" – for framing or for a greeting card front

Or just for colouring!

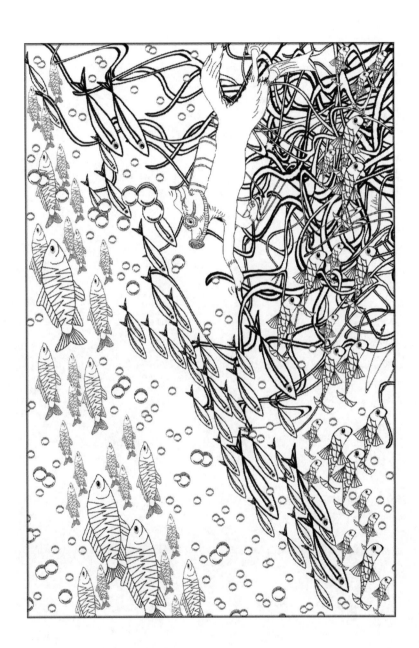

Good Morning, Morning

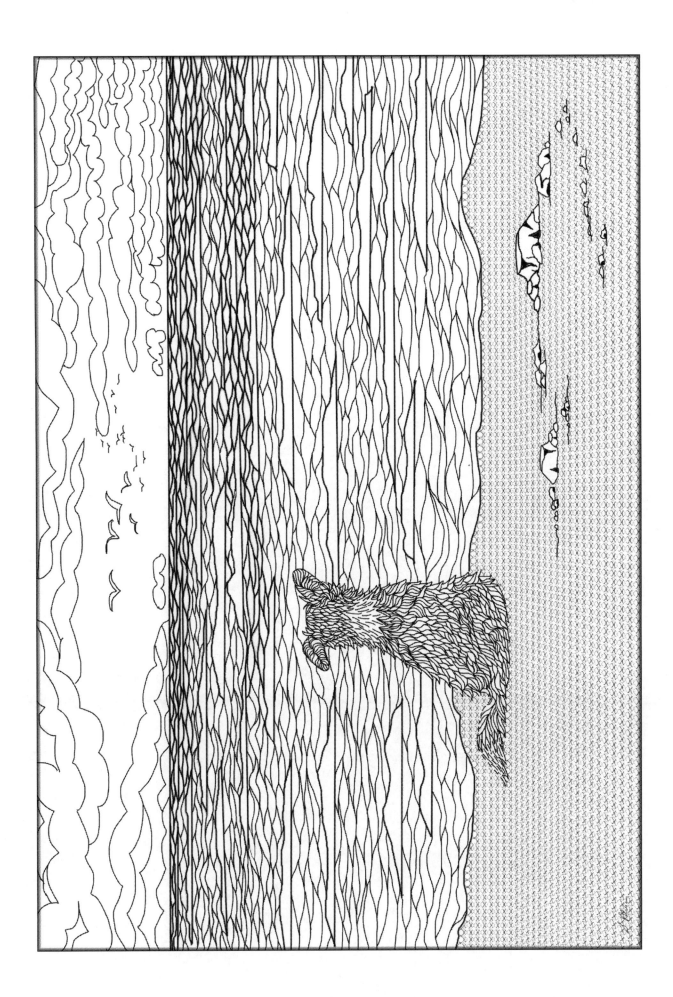

Good Morning, Morning

6"x4" – for framing or for a greeting card front

Or just for colouring!

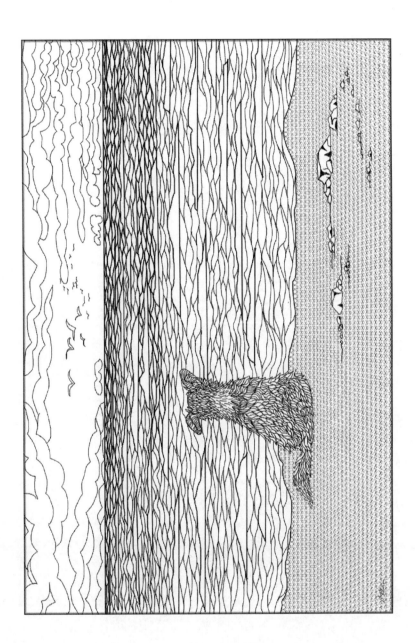

Gardening is fun!

Gardening is fun

6"x4" – for framing or for a greeting card front

Or just for colouring!

Border Collie cycle of life

Thinking of You

Thinking of You

6"x4" – for framing or for a greeting card front

Or just for colouring!

Gottit!

Gottit!

6"x4" – for framing or for a greeting card front

Or just for colouring!

Gottit!

reflections

Gottit!

more reflections

Collieart Nouveau

Collieart Nouveau

6"x4" – for framing or for a greeting card front

Or just for colouring!

He was born to teach

6"x4" – for framing or for a greeting card front

Or just for colouring!

Puppyflies playing with autumn leaves

Puppyflies playing with autumn leaves

6"x4" – for framing or for a greeting card front

Or just for colouring!

Puppyflies playing with autumn leaves

(cropped and enlarged)

Science was his passion

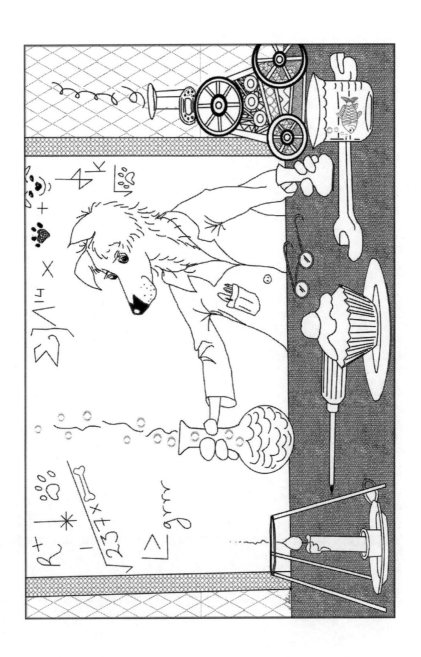

Accountmutt

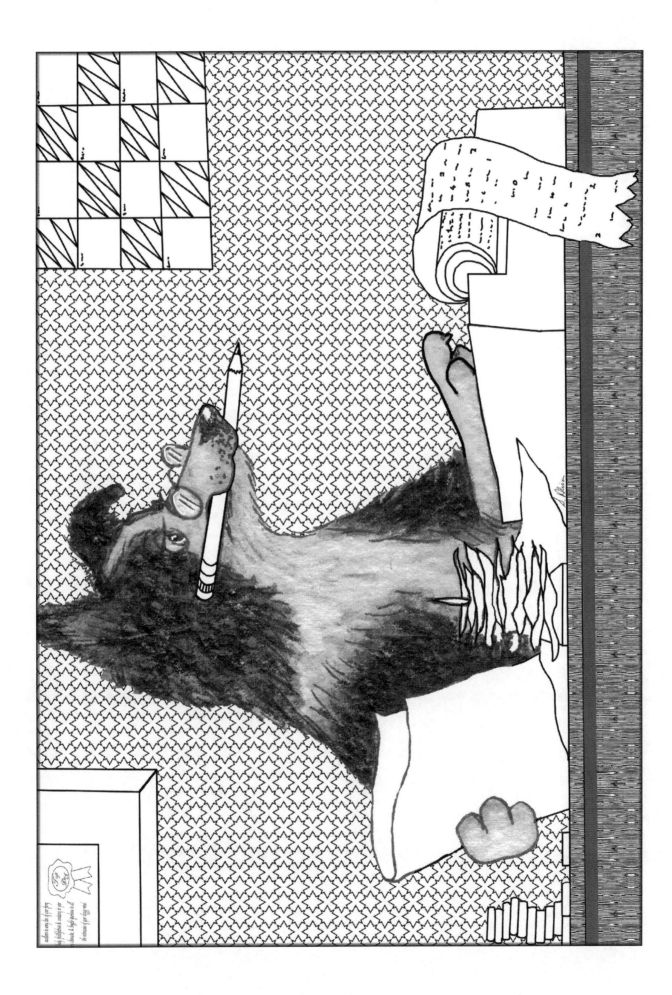

Accountmutt

6"x4" – for framing or for a greeting card front

Or just for colouring!

The answer lies in the soil…

She'd started her Christmas shopping…

She'd started her Christmas shopping...

6"x4" – for framing or for a greeting card front

Or just for colouring!

Starry, starry night

Starry, starry night

6"x4" – for framing or for a greeting card front

Or just for colouring!

Bones across the sky

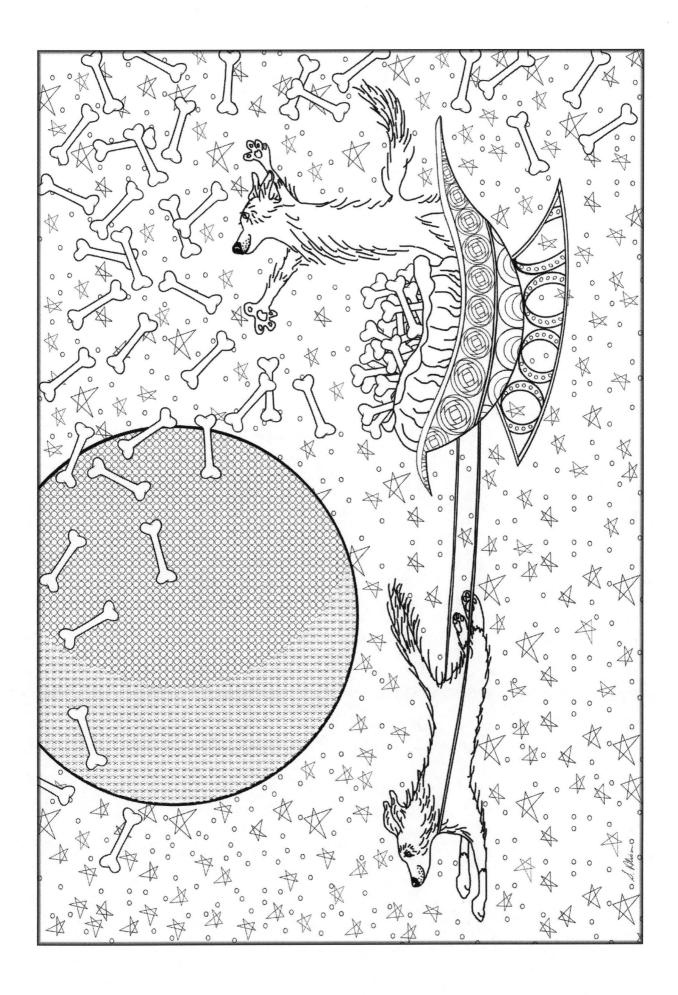

Bones across the sky

6"x4" — for framing or for a greeting card front

Or just for colouring!

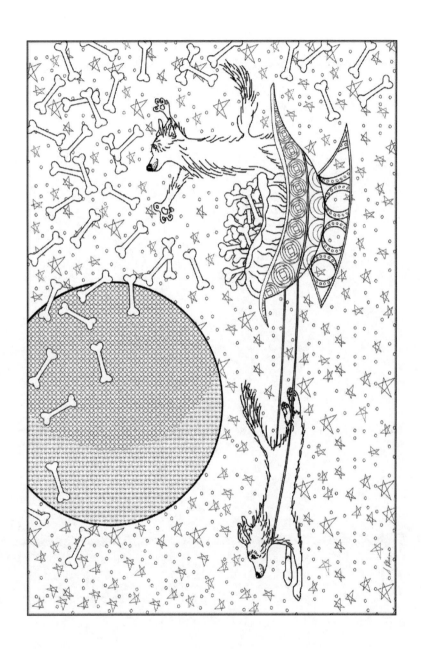

Waiting for Santa

Waiting for Santa

6"x4" – for framing or for a greeting card front

Or just for colouring!

Notepaper for a special person

'Roses'

Notepaper for a special person

'Star flowers'

Notepaper for a special person

'Sheep under the stars'

Bookmarks:

'Butterflies'

'Puppyflies on the roses'

'Sheep under the stars'

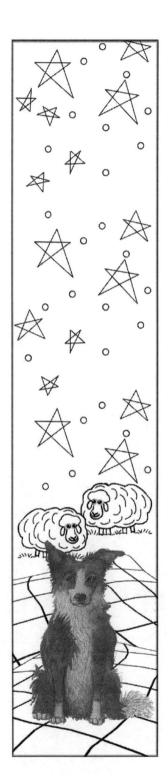

Try out your colours…

A page for trying out your colours:

Try out more colours…

Another page for trying out your colours:

Susan Alison lives in Bristol, UK, and writes and paints full-time. She paints dogs, especially Border Collies, Corgis, Whippets and Greyhounds. Every now and then she paints something that is *not* a dog just to show she's not completely under the paw – mainly, she's under the paw…

Susan's romantic comedies, fantasy novels, colouring books for all ages, illustrated doggerel and short stories can be found on Amazon, Etsy and eBay.

Short stories of hers (*not* usually about dogs) have been published in women's magazines worldwide.

In 2011 she was presented with the Katie Fforde Bursary Award for fiction (with which she's incredibly chuffed).

She has a website at www.SusanAlison.com which features quite a lot of dogs… and if you'd like to receive her (infrequent) newsletter in the comfort of your own inbox, there is a space to put your email address on any of the pages.

Twitter: @bordercollies

Facebook: Susan Alison Art

Also by Susan Alison and available soon…

GREYHOUNDS AND WHIPPETS
Colouring Book (A4 size)
Colouring Book (pocket size)

HOUNDS ABROAD: BOOK THREE
Urban fantasy

The third book starring Lily, Matt and Hounds.

STAKING OUT THE GOAT

Romantic comedy

sequel to the #1 best-selling 'White Lies and Custard Creams'
starring Liz and Moocher.

To receive advance notice of new books you can subscribe
to my newsletter on any page on my website at:
www.SusanAlison.com

Or just email me at Susan@SusanAlison.com
It's always fab to hear from you!

Made in the USA
Middletown, DE
02 October 2017